ᴡᴡ THE STORY OF ᴀᴠ
ALBERT
EINSTEIN

A Biography Book for New Readers

Written by
Susan B. Katz

Illustrated by
Eric Comstock

ROCKRIDGE
PRESS

D0097299

This book is dedicated to the memory of Russell Perrault, a kind soul and creative genius who helped many authors launch their books into the world.

For general information on our other products and services or to obtain technical support, please contact our Customer Care Department within the U.S. at (866) 744-2665, or outside the U.S. at (510) 253-0500.

Rockridge Press publishes its books in a variety of electronic and print formats. Some content that appears in print may not be available in electronic books, and vice versa.

Series Designer: Angela Navarra
Interior and Cover Designer: Angela Navarra
Photo Art Director/Art Manager: Hannah Dickerson
Editor: Kristen Depken
Production Editor: Ashley Polikoff

Illustrations © 2020 Eric Comstock; Creative Market/Semicircular, pp. 2, 11, 16, 21, 31, 38, 42; Alamy Stock Photo/The History Collection, pp. 49, 50; Alamy Stock Photo/History and Art Collection, p. 51. Author photo courtesy of Jeanne Marquis; Illustrator photo courtesy of Kate Comstock.

ISBN: Print 978-1-64611-971-4 | eBook 978-1-64611-974-5

R0

CONTENTS

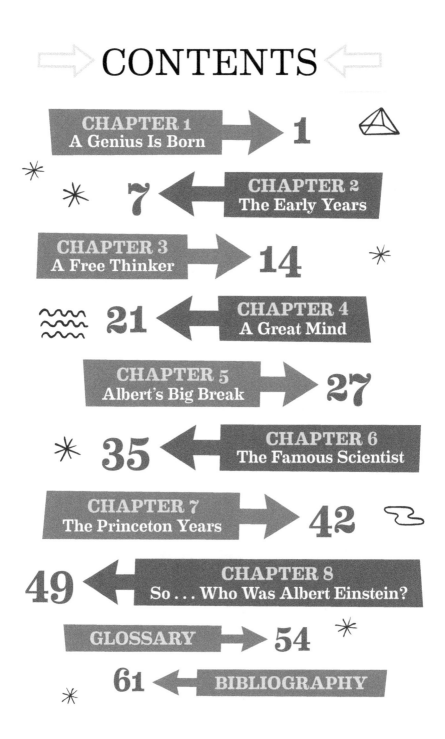

CHAPTER 1

A GENIUS IS BORN

〜〜 Meet Albert Einstein 〜〜

When he was a boy, Albert Einstein didn't speak until he was almost four years old! His parents thought that there might be something wrong with him. So they took Albert to several doctors, who didn't find anything wrong. Albert eventually did speak and, when he grew up, it became clear that he was a **genius**! He had been spending much more time thinking and listening than talking, and he was actually smarter than most other people. After he passed away, his brain was considered so valuable that it was stolen for science! People really wanted to know how a genius's brain works.

When he was alive, Albert looked strange to other people. He didn't comb his hair, wear socks (because he hated when they got holes in them), or have his torn clothing mended. Sometimes people on the street thought he was homeless

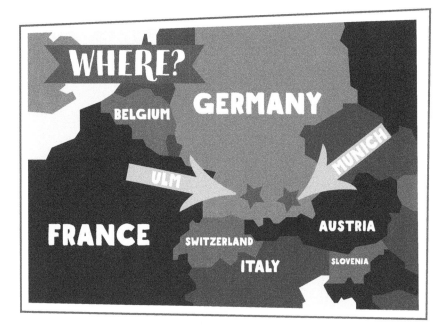

and gave him their food! Albert was simply so focused on thinking and learning that he didn't have time to pay attention to what he wore or how his hair looked. He was too busy discovering his famous **theory of relativity** and important math **equations** like $\mathbf{E=mc^2}$. Albert had a natural **curiosity** about how things worked in the world. From science to math, he loved to solve complex, or difficult, problems with many steps. Albert spent most of his time thinking.

～ Albert's Germany ～

Born on March 14, 1879, in Ulm, Germany, Albert was his parents' first child. When he was just a baby, his family moved to Munich, Germany. When Albert was two, his parents told him that they were going to bring him home something new. Albert thought it would be a toy. When they returned with a new baby sister, Albert was quite disappointed!

Albert loved to build tall houses with playing cards—sometimes up to 14 levels high. Then, he started to play in his father and Uncle Jakob's business, Einstein & Cie, which sold electrical equipment. Albert was fascinated with **electricity** and how it worked. With his father's and uncle's help, he tinkered with batteries and wire, trying to understand how it all connected.

Life was hard for Albert's family. They were Jewish and, at the time, Jews were **discriminated** against in Germany. That meant Jewish people weren't allowed to go to certain schools or open many businesses. But Albert didn't let that stop his natural curiosity about science. He would grow up to be the most important **physicist** of all time!

" **Imagination** is more important than **knowledge.** "

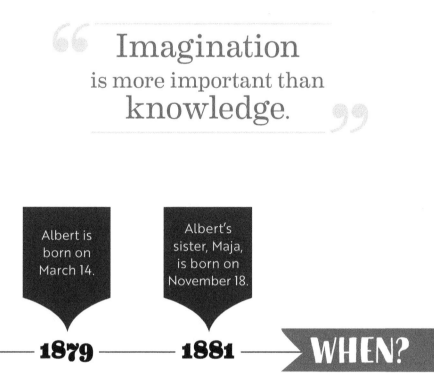

Albert is born on March 14.

Albert's sister, Maja, is born on November 18.

1879 —— 1881 —— **WHEN?**

CHAPTER 2

THE EARLY YEARS

∿∿ Growing Up in Germany ∿∿

When Albert was five, his dad, Hermann, gave him a **compass**, which is a tool used to tell which way you are going (north, south, east, or west). Albert was amazed that it always pointed north, no matter which way he turned it. He was determined to find out how it worked. Albert learned about magnets and Earth's **magnetic field**, which made the needle always point toward the North Pole.

His curiosity and intelligence didn't stop Albert's nanny from nicknaming him "the Dopey One." She watched as he babbled words to himself several times over before saying them out loud. But once his parents knew he was a genius, they asked Albert tough questions about math, science, and the world around them. They encouraged him to ask hard questions, too.

Albert's mother, Pauline, turned him on to the violin. She played piano very well and wanted her son to learn an instrument. At first he had no interest, but after hearing the music of the **composer** Mozart, he decided to learn violin.

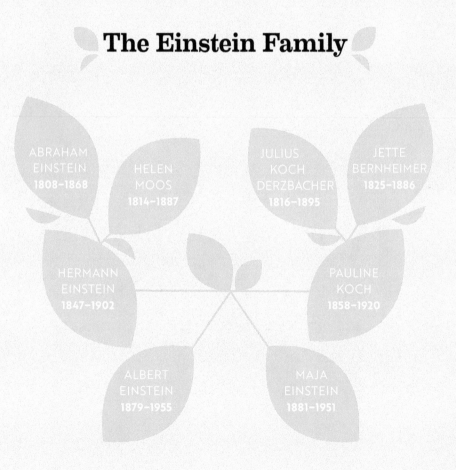

The Einstein Family

ABRAHAM
EINSTEIN
1808–1868

HELEN
MOOS
1814–1887

JULIUS
KOCH
DERZBACHER
1816–1895

JETTE
BERNHEIMER
1825–1886

HERMANN
EINSTEIN
1847–1902

PAULINE
KOCH
1858–1920

ALBERT
EINSTEIN
1879–1955

MAJA
EINSTEIN
1881–1951

Other people in his family encouraged Albert in different ways. His Uncle Jakob taught him advanced math **concepts**, and more about electricity and **magnetism**. Albert began to study how light traveled.

∿∿ School Days ∿∿

Albert liked elementary school and got good grades. But when he started high school at the early age of 10, Albert had very strict teachers who did not want students to ask questions. The children wore uniforms and marched from class to class in lines like soldiers! Albert was bored and did not feel challenged at all.

A family friend named Max Talmey brought Albert books on **geometry**, **chemistry**, and

physics. They were written at the **university** level, but Albert read them all, including, at age 13, Immanuel Kant's *The Critique of Pure Reason.* It made Albert look at the world in a

completely different way. Soon, Max saw that
Albert had passed him in his understanding
of math and physics.

At that time, Albert's father decided to move
his electrical equipment business to Italy. It had
become harder and harder for Jewish people to
live and work in Germany. But they decided to
leave Albert behind to finish high school. Albert

was miserable. He already did not like high school, and now he was all alone. Albert's dislike for his teachers showed through. He spoke out and questioned them so much that he got kicked out of school.

The bright side was that he finally got to join his family in Italy. Albert loved Italy. Eventually, he gave up his German **citizenship** and became a Swiss citizen so that he could attend college in Switzerland, a country next to Italy.

WHEN?

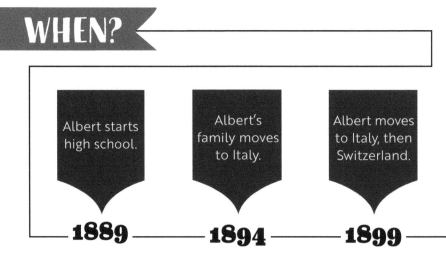

Albert starts high school.

Albert's family moves to Italy.

Albert moves to Italy, then Switzerland.

1889 — **1894** — **1899**

CHAPTER 3

A FREE THINKER

〰 Study Period 〰

Albert fell in love with Italy—its people, music, art, and food. He found Italians to be much friendlier and more **open-minded** than Germans at that time. Finally, Albert was able to read, think, write, explore, and study science. He went on long hikes in the mountains with his sister and, sometimes, on his own. Albert also loved visiting museums and going to concerts.

Many famous scientists interested Albert. Hundreds of years earlier, people had made fun of **astronomers** Galileo and Copernicus for saying that the Earth went around the sun, not the other way around. These scientists argued their **theories**, or scientific ideas, even though everyone thought they were wrong. But they turned out to be very right. Albert found their stories **inspiring**. While he helped out at the family business, he also started writing down some of his own theories and ideas.

In the scientific world, people "publish a paper" in a **journal** for other scientists to read. Albert was still a teenager when he published his first scientific paper.

It was during this time that he decided to go back to school and study physics. The freedom to think became his biggest **priority**. Albert finished high school in Zurich, Switzerland. There, he met close friends who thought on his level, like **mathematician** Marcel Grossmann and Michele Angelo Besso, a Swiss **engineer**.

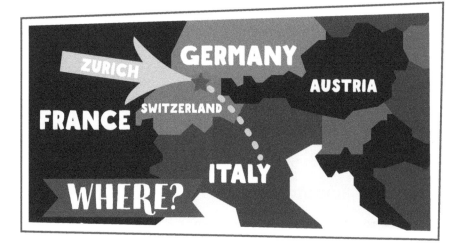

〰 College Days 〰

Albert began college in Zurich. Because his family didn't have much money, an uncle helped pay for his schooling. His high school friend Marcel also lent him all his notes. But Albert still misbehaved a lot in school. Several times, during science **experiments**, he set things in the lab on fire! He also acted like a know-it-all (even around his teachers), which earned him the nickname "Professor." A **professor** is someone who teaches at a university. This was funny because Albert *wanted* to be a professor, and eventually became one.

Albert met his future wife, Mileva Marić (also known as "Dollie"), in college. She was the only woman in his class and was said to be a **prodigy**, a genius since childhood, like Albert. When he graduated from college in 1900, Albert planned

on marrying Mileva and becoming a physics professor. But he couldn't find a job because his teachers wouldn't recommend him. Although he was a genius, people thought of him more as a know-it-all. His uncle stopped giving him money and, sadly, his father passed away. Albert was **devastated**.

Things finally started to look up when Albert's friend Marcel got him a job at the Swiss **patent** office in the city of Bern. The patent office approves **inventions** and makes it illegal for

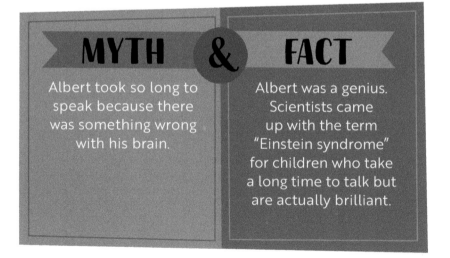

MYTH & **FACT**

Albert took so long to speak because there was something wrong with his brain.

Albert was a genius. Scientists came up with the term "Einstein syndrome" for children who take a long time to talk but are actually brilliant.

other **inventors** to copy those ideas. As a boy, Albert had watched his uncle Jakob apply for six patents. The job was perfect for Albert because many of the patents were about topics that interested him, like electricity. While working at this job, he came up with some of his biggest ideas.

JUMP IN THE THINK TANK

Was there a time in your life when you were feeling unlucky and then someone helped you out or gave you a chance?

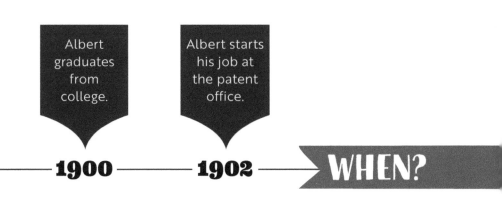

Albert graduates from college.

Albert starts his job at the patent office.

1900 —— **1902** —— **WHEN?**

CHAPTER 4

A GREAT MIND

∼∼∼ **Inventing Ideas** ∼∼∼

Albert liked working at the patent office, and he was good at it. He enjoyed reading about people's ideas and deciding whether to approve them or not. Because Albert was so smart, he was able to finish his patent office work every day with plenty of time left over to work on inventions of his own. If his boss or someone else walked by his desk, he would push his papers aside and act as if he was still working on patents.

WHERE?

BERN

POLAND

CZECH REPUBLIC

GERMANY

AUSTRIA

FRANCE   SWITZERLAND

ITALY

What Albert was really writing had to do with science, math, and very advanced experiments. In just one year, Albert published five scientific papers in a well-known German physics journal. His theories and ideas about science were **groundbreaking**. During his time at the patent office, Albert came up with new theories about electronics, the **atom**, and space travel.

> **A person who never made a mistake never tried anything new.**

∿∿ Family Life ∿∿

Another reason Albert loved his job was because it gave him a regular paycheck. That meant that he could finally marry Mileva and they could start a family. In 1902, Albert and Mileva got married. Two years later, on May 14, 1904, they welcomed their first son, Hans Albert. The Einsteins led a happy life. They took long walks, listened to music, and ate delicious dinners together.

In addition to being husband and wife, Mileva and Albert **collaborated** on a lot of experiments and papers. It is not known exactly which experiments or ideas Mileva came up with and which Albert did, but Albert wrote many letters to Mileva thanking her for helping him. She was **organized** while Albert was not. Even his way of dressing and combing his hair was messy and drew attention. Albert's main focus was thinking. He did not care what he looked like on the outside. To him, it was the mind that mattered. Or, as Albert put it, the inside was more important than the outside.

JUMP IN THE THINK TANK

Why do you think Albert got all the credit for his theories and inventions instead of Mileva getting some credit, too?

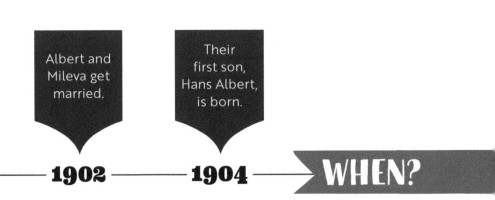

Albert and Mileva get married.

Their first son, Hans Albert, is born.

1902 ——— **1904** ——→ **WHEN?**

~~~ **The Theory of Relativity** ~~~

Albert developed many important theories during his time at the patent office. One major theory that Albert proved was the theory of relativity.

Here's an example of how the theory of relativity works: If two people are playing Ping-Pong on a train that is going 30 miles per hour, to them the ball would look like it is going 2 miles per hour as they hit it back and forth. But, someone standing outside the train would see the ball as going 32 miles per hour (30 + 2)

> There are only two ways to live your life. One is as though nothing is a miracle. The other is as though everything is a miracle.

or 28 miles per hour (30 – 2) if it's being hit the opposite direction that the train is going. To the person outside the train, the ball will always look like it is going in the direction that the train is going, say north. It is all relative to, or depends on, where the person watching the Ping-Pong game is standing. The theory of relativity was Albert's big breakthrough!

After writing this theory, he came up with the most well-known math equation in the world: $E=mc^2$. The "E" stands for **energy**. Albert was saying that the energy of an object is equal to m, its **mass** (how much **matter** an object contains), **multiplied** by c, the speed of light, **squared** (times itself).

Soon, Albert became a very popular teacher, speaker, and rising star in the science world. In 1909, he was offered a job as a professor at the University of Zurich. He and Mileva moved to Zurich, where Mileva soon gave birth to another boy, Eduard. They nicknamed him "Tete," the **Yiddish** word for teddy bear.

~~~ **Back to Germany** ~~~

Over the next few years, the Einsteins moved
many times. They had been in Zurich for less
than a year when Albert decided to take a
different job at a German university in Prague.
Albert was welcomed like a celebrity! He enjoyed
playing violin with a group of musicians in
Prague. But, before long, the Einsteins moved

back to Zurich. Then, Albert was offered another job as a professor in Berlin. Mileva did not want to move back to Germany, so Albert left his wife and sons behind in Zurich. Sadly, Mileva and Albert grew apart and eventually divorced. But he promised that if he ever won a **Nobel Prize**, he would send Mileva and the boys the money that came with the award.

In 1914, Albert settled into Berlin, Germany, to be the director of a physics institute. Soon after, he married a woman named Elsa Löwenthal, who had two girls of her own.

Returning to Germany was hard for Albert. World War I was about to begin. Germany was very unsafe, especially for Jewish people. Albert was focused on his work, but he was also upset about the war. The German government almost put him in jail because he wouldn't support their **violence**.

Through it all, Albert kept working on his theories. One had to do with how light travels. At the time, scientists thought that light traveled in a straight line, but Albert thought that light bends as it travels through space. Albert was right! This was known as **quantum theory**. It became one of Albert's most famous theories, but he didn't like the attention he got from it. He only wanted to focus on continuing his scientific work.

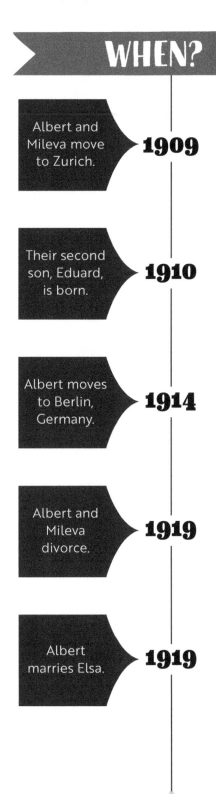

Albert and Mileva move to Zurich.

1909

Their second son, Eduard, is born.

1910

Albert moves to Berlin, Germany.

1914

Albert and Mileva divorce.

1919

Albert marries Elsa.

1919

CHAPTER 6

THE FAMOUS
SCIENTIST

~~~~ Traveling the World ~~~~

As Albert's fame grew, he traveled to speak in other countries. Lots of people, including children, wrote letters to Albert. Some asked if he could help create peace in Germany. World War I had ended, but an evil man named Adolf Hitler rose to power in Germany. He was the leader of the Nazis, who wanted to get rid of all Jewish people. Germany was getting very dangerous for Jewish people as Hitler and the Nazis were taking over. Albert spoke out against them. His new wife, Elsa, was afraid that would

> Learn from yesterday, live for today, hope for tomorrow. The important thing is to not stop questioning.

put him in danger, but Albert did not care. He was Jewish and wanted to use his fame to better the world.

Albert took trips to Israel to help start a new Jewish state so Jewish people could escape Germany safely. In 1921, he traveled to the United States, where he worked with other important people to raise money for the Jewish homeland. He was greeted by reporters and

photographers. The mayor of New York City even presented him with a key to the city. Elsa gave him a comb for his messy hair and told him to dress better, but Albert ignored her advice. The American people loved Albert's wild look.

Over the years, Albert had been **nominated** for the Nobel Prize seven times without winning. Then, in 1922, he finally won for his thinking about the **photoelectric effect,** or how light bends. This work would eventually lead to the invention of the television! As promised, Albert sent Mileva and the boys the money that came with the prize. The award also gave Albert even more fame and attention.

∿∿∿ **Working for Peace** ∿∿∿

Unfortunately, Hitler and the Nazis took control of Germany in the early 1930s. More and more, Albert risked his life by speaking out against them. The Nazis said he was a spy and **threatened**

to kill him. They burned his books. Not only was Albert Jewish, he was very **outspoken** against the Nazis and their violent ways.

When Albert and Elsa were away in California, where Albert was speaking as a visiting professor, the Nazis broke into their home. Soon it became too dangerous for Albert to stay in

Germany. He and Elsa moved to
Belgium. Albert continued traveling
and speaking in other countries.
In Spain, the king greeted him.
Japan made the day he arrived a
national holiday.

JUMP IN THE THINK TANK

Why do you think Albert was called a spy by the Nazis? Why did he continue to speak out against them anyway?

Everywhere Albert went, people loved him—except in his homeland of Germany. In 1933, he was offered a job teaching math in Princeton, New Jersey. He and Elsa decided to move to the United States for good. A few years later, World War II began. By the time it ended, millions of Jewish people were killed by the Nazis in the **Holocaust**. Albert and Elsa felt lucky to have escaped when they did.

WHEN?

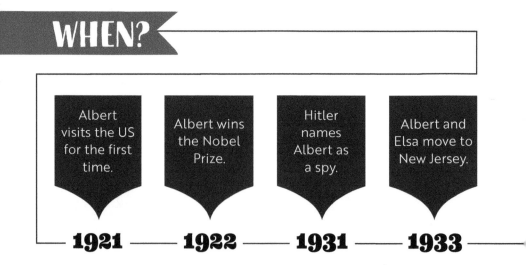

Albert visits the US for the first time.

Albert wins the Nobel Prize.

Hitler names Albert as a spy.

Albert and Elsa move to New Jersey.

1921 — **1922** — **1931** — **1933**

CHAPTER 7

THE PRINCETON YEARS

〰 The Atomic Bomb 〰

Albert's life in the United States wasn't easy. He was given the chance to teach at one of the most **prestigious** schools in the country, Princeton University in New Jersey. But Albert did not speak English. At first, when he was asked to give a **lecture**, speaking to a group of students about his work, he would write the whole thing in German and have someone else **translate** it into English. Learning a language later in life is difficult, but Albert did it anyway. He eventually learned to write and speak in English.

Sadly, after three years of living in New Jersey, Elsa passed away. Then Albert got quite ill with stomach problems. He was also very upset by what was happening in Germany. Albert was very much against World War II. He continued to fight against Hitler and the Nazis as best he could. When he heard about friends being killed in Germany, he decided he had to do something about it.

On August 2, 1939, Albert and another scientist named Leó Szilárd wrote an important

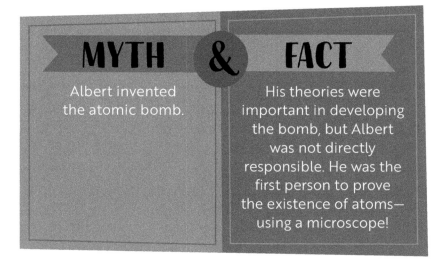

letter to United States President Franklin D. Roosevelt. In the letter, they warned the president that the Nazis in Germany were developing an **atomic bomb** that could harm many people. Partly because of this letter, the United States also began to develop an atomic bomb. After World War II began, Albert wrote the president a second time with concerns about the bomb. Unfortunately, the president died the same year and probably never saw Albert's letter. In 1945, the United States dropped two atomic bombs on Japan to end World War II.

~~~ **A Peaceful Life** ~~~

Albert was very upset that his research helped create something so dangerous. After the war, he worked for peace and tried to stop others from using atomic weapons. In 1940, he became a United States citizen, but he also kept his Swiss citizenship. Albert's first wife, Mileva, still lived in Switzerland with their son, Eduard. Their other son, Hans Albert, moved to California. He and Albert were able to visit each other from time to time.

Do you have a special space where you can work quietly and focus? How does that help you get work done and think more clearly?

Albert retired from his job at Princeton in 1945, but kept an office there for the rest of his life. Albert's last years were peaceful and happy. He was able to focus on his ideas. He loved going on walks around Princeton, sailing (even though

he couldn't swim), and playing the violin. He
also enjoyed spending time with his sister, Maja,
who came to live with him in Princeton.

In 1948, Albert was glad when the state of
Israel was formed as a Jewish homeland. He
had been working toward this safe place for
Jewish people for years. Albert was even asked

to be its president. He said no, but he was honored by the offer.

Albert had become very ill and, on April 18, 1955, he died while working on new equations. Albert left his important scientific papers to the Hebrew University in Israel. He left his violin to his grandson Bernhard. During his life, Albert published more than 300 scientific papers. There is even a metal, einsteinium, named after Albert. His famous theories live on today and have changed our world!

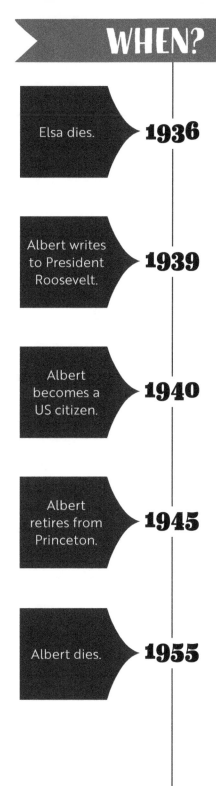

Elsa dies. **1936**

Albert writes to President Roosevelt. **1939**

Albert becomes a US citizen. **1940**

Albert retires from Princeton. **1945**

Albert dies. **1955**

CHAPTER 8

SO ... WHO WAS ALBERT EINSTEIN?

~~~ **Challenge Accepted!** ~~~

Now that you know so much about Albert's life and work, let's test your new knowledge in a little who, what, when, where, why, and how quiz. Feel free to look back in the text to find the answers if you need to, but try to remember first!

1 **Where was Albert born?**

→ A   Zurich, Switzerland
→ B   Princeton, New Jersey
→ C   Ulm, Germany
→ D   Milan, Italy

2 **What theory is Albert most famous for?**

→ A   The theory of relativity
→ B   The theory of how to dress messy
→ C   The theory of train travel
→ D   The theory of space and time

3 **What were Albert's wives' names?**

→ A   Margaret and Elizabeth
→ B   Mileva and Elsa
→ C   Marji and Elly
→ D   Mo and Curly

4 **What were some of Albert's most notable accomplishments?**

 A Walking on the moon and winning an Oscar

→ B Writing a book and discovering dinosaurs

→ C Juggling and wood carving

→ D Discovering that light bends and the equation $E=mc^2$

5 **What did Albert's father give him that first got him interested in magnetism?**

→ A A compass

→ B A yo-yo

→ C A cell phone

→ D A bicycle

6 **Where was Albert's first official job before becoming a professor?**

→ A In his dad's ice-cream shop

→ B In a planetarium

→ C In a patent office

→ D In a barber shop

7 How many times was Albert nominated for a Nobel Prize before he won?

→ A   Five
→ B   Seven
→ C   One hundred
→ D   One

8 In what year did Albert win the Nobel Prize?

→ A   1922
→ B   1955
→ C   1909
→ D   2020

9 What instrument did Albert play?

→ A   The clarinet
→ B   The flute
→ C   The piano
→ D   The violin

10 At which university did Albert spend the end of his career as a professor?

→ A   Berlin University
→ B   Stanford University
→ C   Princeton University
→ D   The University of Michigan

～～ Our World ～～

Albert Einstein's work changed the way people think about many scientific ideas. Let's look at a few things that are different because of Albert's genius discoveries.

→ Scientists all over the globe now look differently at light and how it bends. Einstein's discoveries about light led to many inventions, including the television.

→ Discoveries do not happen overnight! Einstein worked for 10 years on the theory of relativity. It changed the way we view the world and gave future scientists hope that, even if something seems like a crazy theory, it might just be right!

→ Because of Einstein's theories about space and time, scientists today are better able to study black holes far away in space.

→ Albert fought for peace and is even considered to be like the famous **pacifist** Gandhi in his desire to stop violence. He warned President Harry S. Truman that the atomic bomb could destroy humankind as we know it.

JUMP IN THE THINK TANK FOR MORE!

Let's think a little more deeply about how Albert's daring discoveries affected the world we live in today.

→ What kinds of science classes do you take in school? Have you ever come up with a theory, or new idea, and tested it to see if you were right?

→ Who are some scientists you know of? Do you have any role models who are physicists, like Albert, or other kinds of scientists?

→ What are some ways to promote peace in your community? When there is talk of war, what can people do to peacefully voice their opinions like Albert did?

Glossary

astronomers: Scientists who study the stars, planets, and solar system

atom: The smallest unit of matter

atomic bomb: An explosive device with extreme power to destroy through heat, blast, and radioactivity

chemistry: The study of the substances that make up matter and how they interact

citizenship: When a person legally lives in and belongs to a country, regardless of whether they are born there or move there later in life

collaborated: Worked together on a project

compass: A tool with a magnetized pointer that shows the direction of magnetic north and helps people figure out what direction they're going

composer: A person who writes music, especially as their job

concepts: Ideas formed based on evidence

curiosity: A strong desire to know or learn something

devastated: Very shocked or upset

discriminated: Treated unfairly or differently because of one's race, sex, religion, or age

E=mc²: Albert Einstein's famous math equation that shows that the energy of an object is equal to its mass times the speed of light squared

electricity: A form of energy that comes from charged particles

engineer: A person who designs or builds machines

energy: The potential or power of a person or object to move, change, or make things happen

equation: A mathematical statement in which two things are equal

experiment: A procedure that scientists perform to try to make a discovery or prove a theory

genius: A person who is unusually intelligent

geometry: The mathematical study of shapes, planes, and figures

groundbreaking: New and different in a way that changes how people think about something

Holocaust: The mass killing of more than six million Jewish people and others by Hitler's Nazis in Europe during World War II (1941 to 1945)

inspiring: Filling someone with the desire or ability to do or feel something, especially to do something creative

invention: Something new that has never been made before

inventor: A person who creates and discovers new things

journal: A magazine in the science world, medical field, or other professional arena

lecture: The event of formally speaking to a group of students in order to teach something

magnetic field: An area or space around magnetic material within which the force of magnetism acts

magnetism: A force that causes objects to be pulled together or pushed apart

mass: The amount of matter or substance that makes up an object

mathematician: Someone who studies math

matter: Anything that takes up space and has mass

multiplied: Increased in number by a certain amount

Nobel Prize: An international prize awarded every year for outstanding work in physics, chemistry, medicine, literature, economics, or the promotion of peace

nominated: Suggested as the possible winner of an award or prize

open-minded: Willing to accept the possibility of new ideas or try new things

organized: Having things in order, or in a system, to deal with them more easily

outspoken: Open in stating opinions and ideas

pacifist: Someone who opposes war or violence and promotes peace

patent: A document that gives someone the right to make, use, or sell an invention and prevents others from copying it

photoelectric effect: The release of electrons from a metal surface when light hits it

physicist: A person who studies matter, energy, and how they interact

physics: The study of matter, energy, and the interaction between them

prestigious: Well-known and well-respected; having high status

priority: Something more important than other things

prodigy: A person, especially a young one, who shows very advanced skills in music, science, math, or another field

professor: A teacher at the university or college level

quantum theory: A theory that explains how matter and energy behave on the very small level of atoms and molecules

squared: When a number is multiplied by itself (for example, 5 squared means 5 x 5 = 25)

theory: An idea about something that a scientist tries to prove. The plural of theory is **theories**.

theory of relativity: Einstein's idea about how the nature of things depends on who is viewing them and from where

threatened: Told that someone is going to harm you

translate: To change words from one language to another

university: A college or place of higher learning

violence: The use of physical force to harm someone or something

Yiddish: A language that combines Hebrew and German and was originally spoken by Eastern European Jewish people

Bibliography

Calaprice, Alice and Evelyn Einstein. *Dear Professor Einstein*. New York: Prometheus Books, 2002.

Ducksters Education Site. "Physics for Kids: Theory of Relativity." Accessed January 2, 2020. Ducksters.com/science/physics/theory_of_relativity.php.

Einstein, Albert. *Autobiographical Notes*. La Salle, Illinois: Open Court, 1996.

Folsing, Albrecht. *Albert Einstein: A Biography*. New York: Viking, 1997.

Getty Images. *Albert Einstein, Theoretical Physicist, and His Sister Maja as Small Children*. Accessed January 11, 2020. GettyImages.com/detail/news -photo/albert-einstein-theoretical-physicist-and-his-sister-maja-news-photo /463909645.

GP Editors. *My Life: Albert Einstein*. New Delhi, India: General Press, 2018.

Johnson, M. Alex. "The Culture of Einstein." NBC News. Accessed January 14, 2020. NBCnews.com/id/7406337/ns/technology_and_science -science/t/culture-einstein/#.Xh33Ohd7mgQ.

Silen, Andrea. "Albert Einstein." *National Geographic Kids* online. Accessed December 20, 2019. Kids.NationalGeographic.com/explore/history/albert -einstein.

Yeatts, Tabatha. *Albert Einstein: The Miracle Mind*. New York: Sterling Publishing, 2007.

Acknowledgments

First and foremost, I want to thank Albert Einstein for defending Jewish people during World War II and for his brilliance in challenging the status quo in science. It was an inspiration and an honor to research and write about him. I appreciate my outstanding editor, Kristen, who entrusted me with this book and guided me with clarity, precision, and determination. I appreciate my parents, Janice and Ray, for their encouragement. Thanks also to my brother, Steve, for his support. Kudos to my talented writers' group—Andrew, Brandi, Evan, Kyle, and Sonia. In memory of my Grandma Grace and my Aunt Judy. To my nephews, Sam, Jacob, and David, and my nieces, Sofia and Katherine. Thanks to the entire Callisto team! I am supported by family and friends: Michelle G., Susan, Ann and Greg, Danielle, Jeanne, Deborah, Kiernan, Laurie, Tanya, Carla, Julia and Ira, Maureen, Amparo, Michael, Ricardo, Alejandra, Arden, Jen, Tami, Karen, Annie, Crystal, Bryan, Jessica, Marji, Marcy, Lara, Anita and Bob, Jerry, Nena and Mel, Jami, Stacy and Rick, Laura and Darren, Michelle R., Chalmers, Violeta, Diana y Juanca, and Sylvia Boorstein.

—SBK

About the Author

SUSAN B. KATZ is an award-winning bilingual author, National Board Certified Teacher, educational consultant, and keynote speaker. She taught for over 25 years. Susan has published books with Scholastic, Random House, Barefoot Books, and Bala Books. Her titles include *Meditation Station*, *ABC Baby Me!*, *My Mama Earth* (Moonbeam Gold Award Winner for Best Picture Book and named "Top Green Toy" by Education.com), *ABC School's For Me* (illustrated by Lynn Munsinger), and *All Year Round*, which she translated into Spanish as *Un Año Redondo*. She also authored *The Story of Ruth Bader Ginsburg*, *The Story of Frida Kahlo*, and *The Story of Jane Goodall* for Callisto Media. Susan is the executive director of ConnectingAuthors.org, a national nonprofit that brings children's book authors and illustrators into schools. Ms. Katz served as the strategic partner manager for authors at Facebook. When she's not writing, Susan enjoys traveling, salsa dancing, and spending time at the beach. You can find out more about her books and school visits at **SusanKatzBooks.com**.

About the Illustrator

ERIC COMSTOCK has co-authored and illustrated the Charlie Piechart books. He also illustrated *The Great Dictionary Caper* by Judy Sierra, which received starred reviews from *Booklist* and *Kirkus Reviews*. When Eric isn't illustrating picture books he works as a creative director at an advertising firm in Salt Lake City, where he lives with his family.

WHO WILL INSPIRE YOU NEXT?

EXPLORE A WORLD OF HEROES AND ROLE MODELS IN
THE STORY OF... BIOGRAPHY SERIES FOR NEW READERS.

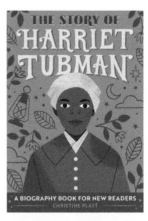

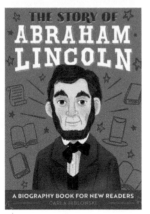

LOOK FOR THIS SERIES
WHEREVER BOOKS AND EBOOKS ARE SOLD

Alexander Hamilton

Albert Einstein

Martin Luther King Jr.

George Washington

Jane Goodall

Barack Obama

Helen Keller

Marie Curie